MW00980226

Calling
on
the
Name
of
the Lord

Witness Lee

Living Stream Ministry
Anaheim, California • www.lsm.org

ISBN 978-1-57593-383-2

Living Stream Ministry

2431 W. La Palma Ave., Anaheim, CA 92801
P. O. Box 2121, Anaheim, CA 92814 USA

14 15 16 17 / 11 10 9 8 7

CALLING ON THE
NAME OF THE LORD

What is the meaning of calling on the name of the Lord? Some Christians think that calling on the Lord is the same as praying to Him. Yes, calling is a kind of prayer, but it is not merely praying. The Hebrew word for *call* means to call out to, to cry unto, to cry out. The Greek word for *call* means to invoke a person, to call a person by name. In other words, it is to call a person by naming him audibly. Although prayer may be silent, calling must be audible.

Two Old Testament prophets help us to see what is meant by calling on the Lord. Jeremiah tells us that to call on the Lord means to cry to Him and to experience spiritual breathing. "I called upon Your name, O Jehovah, from the lowest pit. You have heard my voice; do not hide Your ear at my breathing, at my cry" (Lam. 3:55-56). Isaiah also tells us that our calling on the Lord is our crying to Him. "God is now my salvation; I will trust and not dread; for Jah Jehovah is my strength and song, and He has become my salvation. Therefore you will draw water with rejoicing from the springs of salvation, and you will say in that day, Praise Jehovah; call upon His name!...Sing to Jehovah.... Cry out and give a ringing shout, O inhabitant of Zion, for great in your midst is the Holy One of Israel" (Isa. 12:2-6). How may God become our salvation, our strength, and our song? How can we draw water with rejoicing from the springs of salvation? The way is to call on His name, to praise the Lord, to sing a hymn, and to cry out and shout. All of these match the calling mentioned in verse 4!

CALLING ON THE NAME OF THE LORD IN THE OLD TESTAMENT

Calling on the Lord began in the third generation of the human race with Enosh, the son of Seth (Gen. 4:26). The history of calling on the Lord's name continued throughout the Bible with Abraham (Gen. 12:8), Isaac (Gen. 26:25), Moses (Deut. 4:7), Job (Job 12:4), Jabez (1 Chron. 4:10),

Samson (Judg. 16:28), Samuel (1 Sam. 12:18), David (2 Sam. 22:4), Jonah (Jonah 1:6), Elijah (1 Kings 18:24), and Jeremiah (Lam. 3:55). Not only did the Old Testament saints call on the Lord, they even prophesied that others would call on His name (Joel 2:32; Zeph. 3:9; Zech. 13:9). Although many are familiar with Joel's prophecy regarding the Holy Spirit, not many have paid attention to the fact that receiving the outpoured Holy Spirit requires our calling on the name of the Lord. On the one hand, Joel prophesied that God would pour out His Spirit; on the other hand, he prophesied that people would call on the name of the Lord. This prophecy was fulfilled on the day of Pentecost (Acts 2:17a, 21). God's outpouring needs the cooperation of our calling on Him.

PRACTICED BY
NEW TESTAMENT BELIEVERS

Calling on the name of the Lord was practiced by the New Testament believers beginning on the day of Pentecost (Acts 2:21). While Stephen was being stoned to death, he was calling on the name of the Lord (Acts 7:59). The New Testament believers practiced calling on the Lord (Acts 9:14; 22:16; 1 Cor. 1:2; 2 Tim. 2:22). Saul of Tarsus received authority from the chief priests to bind all that called on the name of the Lord (Acts 9:14). This indicates that all the early saints were Jesus-callers. Their calling on the name of the Lord was a sign, a mark, that they were Christians. If we become those who call on the name of the Lord, our calling will mark us out as Christians.

Paul the apostle stressed the matter of calling when he wrote the book of Romans. He said, "For there is no distinction between Jew and Greek, for the same Lord is Lord of all and rich to all who call upon Him; for whoever calls upon the name of the Lord shall be saved" (Rom. 10:12-13). Paul also spoke of calling on the Lord in 1 Corinthians when he wrote the words, "With all those who call upon the name of our Lord Jesus Christ in every place, who is theirs and ours" (1 Cor. 1:2). Furthermore, in 2 Timothy he told Timothy to pursue spiritual things with those who call on the Lord out of a pure heart (2:22). By all of these verses we can see that in the first century the Christians practiced calling on the name of the Lord very much. Therefore, throughout the Old Testament as well as in the early days of the Christian age, the saints called on the Lord's name. How regrettable that it has been neglected by most Christians for so long a time. We believe that today the Lord wants to recover calling on His name and to have us practice it so that we may enjoy the riches of His life.

THE PURPOSE OF CALLING

Why do we need to call on the name of the Lord? Men need to call on the name of the Lord in order to be saved (Rom. 10:13). The way of praying quietly does help people to be saved, but not so richly. The way of calling loudly helps people to be saved in a richer and more thorough way. Thus, we need to encourage people to open themselves and to call on the name of the Lord Jesus. Psalm 116 tells us that we may partake of the Lord's salvation by calling on Him: "I will take the cup of salvation, and call upon the name of the

Lord" (v. 13). In this one Psalm, calling on the Lord is mentioned four times (vv. 2, 4, 13, 17). As we have seen earlier, the way to draw water from the springs of salvation is to call upon the name of the Lord (Isa. 12:2-4). Many Christians have never called upon the Lord. If you have never called, even shouted before the Lord, it is doubtful that you have enjoyed the Lord in a rich way. "Call upon His name!...Cry out and give a ringing shout" (Isa. 12:4, 6). Try shouting before Him. If you have never shouted about what the Lord is to you, try it. The more you shout, "O Lord Jesus, You are so good to me!" the more you will be released from your self and filled with the Lord. Thousands of saints have been released and enriched through calling on the name of the Lord.

Another reason for calling on the Lord is to be rescued from distress (Psa. 18:6; 118:5), from trouble (Psa. 50:15; 86:7; 81:7), and from sorrow and pain (Psa. 116:3-4). People who have argued against calling on the Lord have found themselves calling on Him when they were subject to a certain trouble or illness. When our lives are free from trouble, we may argue against calling on the Lord. However, when trouble comes, no one will need to tell us to call on Him; we will call spontaneously.

Also, the way for us to participate in the Lord's plenteous mercy is to call upon Him. The more we call upon Him, the more we enjoy His mercy (Psa. 86:5). Another reason for calling on the Lord is to receive the Spirit (Acts 2:17a, 21). The best and easiest way to be filled with the Holy Spirit is to call on the name of the Lord Jesus. The Spirit has already been poured out. We simply need to receive Him by calling on the Lord.

Isaiah 55:1 says, "Ho! Everyone who thirsts, come to the waters, and you who have no money; come, buy and eat; yes, come, buy wine and milk without money and without price." What is the way to eat and drink the Lord? Isaiah gives us the way in verse 6 of the same chapter: "Seek Jehovah while He may be found; call upon Him while He is near." Thus, the way to eat the spiritual food for our satisfaction is to seek the Lord and to call upon His name.

Romans 10:12 says that the Lord of all is rich to all who call upon Him. The way to enjoy the riches of the Lord is to call upon Him. The Lord is not only rich, but also near and available, because He is the life-giving Spirit (1 Cor. 15:45b). As the Spirit, He is omnipresent. We may call on His name at any time and in any place. When we call on Him, He comes to us as the Spirit, and we enjoy His riches.

First Corinthians is a book on the enjoyment of Christ. In chapter twelve, Paul tells us how to enjoy Him. The way to enjoy the Lord is to call on His name (12:3; 1:2). Whenever we call "Lord Jesus," He comes as the Spirit, and we drink of Him (12:13), the life-giving Spirit. If I call a person's name, and if he is real, living, and present, that person will come to me. The Lord Jesus is real, living, and present! He is always available. Whenever we call on Him, He comes. Do you want to enjoy the Lord's presence with all His riches? The best way to experience His presence with all His riches is to call on His name. Call on Him while you are driving on the freeway or while you are at work. Anywhere and anytime you may call. The Lord is near and rich to you.

Also, by calling on the name of the Lord, we can stir ourselves up. Isaiah 64:7 says, "And there is no one who calls upon Your name, who stirs himself up to lay hold of You." When we feel that we are down or low, we can lift and stir ourselves up by calling on the name of the Lord Jesus.

THE WAY TO CALL

How should we call on the Lord? We must call on Him out of a pure heart (2 Tim. 2:22). Our heart, which is the source of our calling, must be pure, seeking nothing except the Lord Himself. Also, we must call with a pure lip (Zeph. 3:9). We need to watch our speech, for nothing contaminates our lips more than loose talk. If our lips are impure due to loose talk, it will be difficult for us to call on the Lord. Along with a pure heart and pure lips, we need to have an open mouth (Psa. 81:10). We need to open our mouth wide to call on the Lord. Furthermore, we need to call on the Lord corporately. Second Timothy 2:22

says, "But flee youthful lusts, and pursue righteousness, faith, love, peace with those who call on the Lord out of a pure heart." We need to come together for the purpose of calling on the name of the Lord. Psalm 88:9 says, "Lord, I have called daily upon thee." Hence, we should call daily upon His name. Furthermore, Psalm 116:2 says, "Therefore will I call upon him as long as I live." As long as we live, we should call on the name of the Lord.

THE NEED OF PRACTICE

Calling on the name of the Lord is not merely a doctrine. It is very practical. We need to practice it daily and hourly. We should never stop our spiritual breathing. We hope that many more of the Lord's people, especially new believers, will begin the practice of calling on the Lord. Today, many Christians have found that they can know Him, that they can be brought into the power of His resurrection, that they can experience His spontaneous salvation, and that they can walk in oneness with Him by calling on His name. In any situation, at any time, call: "Lord Jesus,

O Lord Jesus!" If you practice calling on His name, you will see that it is a wonderful way to enjoy the Lord's riches.